WHAT DO CALL ME?

A BOOK OF CUTE AND FUNNY BABY ANIMALS

AGES 2-8

FROM ANIMAL WONDERS:
A SERIES OF BOOKS ABOUT AMAZING AND ADORABLE ANIMALS

This book was written and illustrated by José Marques
Copyright © 2023 by José Pedro Fernandes Marques. All rights reserved

WHAT DO YOU CALL A BABY BEAR?
A BEAR CUB!

A BEAR CUB IS FUZZY AND CUDDLY, BUT WATCH OUT!
IT WILL GROW UP TO BE BIG AND STRONG.

DID YOU KNOW THAT A BEAR CUB CAN CLIMB TREES VERY WELL?
BUT IT HAS TO COME DOWN BACKWARDS. THAT'S TRICKY!

A BEAR CUB ALSO HAS A SUPER NOSE.
IT CAN SMELL THINGS FROM VERY FAR AWAY,
EVEN IF THEY ARE BURIED UNDER SNOW. SNIFF!
CAN YOU SMELL THAT HONEY? YUM!

WHAT DO YOU CALL A BABY SQUIRREL?
A PUP, KIT OR KITTEN!

IT HAS FUR AND A BUSHY TAIL, BUT IT CAN'T CLIMB OR JUMP YET.
IT STAYS WITH ITS MOMMY AND SIBLINGS IN A HOLE OR A NEST.

DID YOU KNOW THAT A PUP CAN STORE FOOD FOR LATER?
IT DOES THIS BY BURYING NUTS AND SEEDS IN THE GROUND
IT LIKES TO EAT NUTS, SEEDS AND FRUITS. CRUNCH!

A PUP ALSO HAS A VERY CURIOUS PERSONALITY.
SOMETIMES IT EXPLORES NEW THINGS WITH ITS PAWS OR TEETH.
CAN YOU EXPLORE LIKE A BABY SQUIRREL?

WHAT DO YOU CALL A BABY ELEPHANT?
AN ELEPHANT CALF!

AN ELEPHANT CALF IS VERY BIG AND HEAVY,
EVEN BIGGER THAN A GROWN-UP HUMAN!

AN ELEPHANT CALF ALSO HAS A LONG TRUNK.
BUT IT HAS TO LEARN HOW TO USE IT FIRST.
SOMETIMES IT TRIPS ON ITS TRUNK OR GETS IT TANGLED WITH OTHER THINGS.

IT CAN ALSO MAKE A LOUD TRUMPET SOUND
TO COMMUNICATE WITH OTHER ELEPHANTS.
TRUMPET!
CAN YOU MAKE A SOUND LIKE AN ELEPHANT? HONK!

WHAT DO YOU CALL A BABY HIPPO?
A HIPPO CALF!

A CALF IS BORN FROM A VERY BIG MOMMY.
IT IS THE BIGGEST BABY IN THE WATER!
IT HAS THICK SKIN AND SHORT LEGS, BUT IT CAN SWIM VERY WELL.

A CALF ALSO HAS A VERY FUNNY HABIT.
SOMETIMES IT OPENS ITS MOUTH VERY WIDE
TO SHOW OFF ITS TEETH OR TO YAWN.
BUT IT CAN STILL SEE AND HEAR WHAT'S GOING ON AROUND IT.
CAN YOU OPEN YOUR MOUTH LIKE A BABY HIPPO?

WHAT DO YOU CALL A BABY KANGAROO?

A JOEY!

A JOEY IS A TINY BABY. IT IS SO SMALL THAT IT CAN FIT IN A TEASPOON.
IT HAS NO FUR AND ITS EYES ARE CLOSED.
IT CRAWLS INTO ITS MOTHER'S POUCH, WHERE IT STAYS FOR A LONG TIME.

A JOEY CAN HAVE A BIG BROTHER OR SISTER
THAT CAN HOP IN AND OUT OF THE POUCH. HOP!

CAN YOU JUMP LIKE A KANGAROO?
BOING!

WHAT DO YOU CALL A BABY HEDGEHOG?
A HOGLET!

A HOGLET IS BORN WITH SOFT SPINES THAT HARDEN AFTER A FEW HOURS. IT CAN ROLL INTO A BALL TO PROTECT ITSELF.

DID YOU KNOW THAT A HEDGEHOG
HAS MORE SPINES THAN ANY OTHER ANIMAL?
THAT'S AMAZING! WOW!

A HOGLET ALSO LIKES TO SWIM AND PLAY IN THE WATER. SPLASH!
CAN YOU JOIN A HOGLET FOR A SWIM?

WHAT DO YOU CALL A BABY PARROT?
A PARROT CHICK!

A PARROT CHICK IS BORN WITH ONLY A FEW FLUFFY FEATHERS.
IT NEEDS ITS MOMMY OR DADDY TO FEED IT AND KEEP IT WARM.

DID YOU KNOW THAT SOME PARROT CHICKS
CAN TALK LIKE PEOPLE WHEN THEY ARE STILL BABIES?
THEY LEARN BY COPYING THEIR PARENTS AND OTHER SOUNDS AROUND THEM.

SQUAWK! CAN YOU TALK TO A PARROT CHICK?
HELLO!

WHAT DO YOU CALL A BABY SKUNK?
A SKUNK KIT!

A KIT IS BORN WITH BLACK AND WHITE FUR,
JUST LIKE ITS MOMMY AND DADDY.

DID YOU KNOW THAT A SKUNK CAN SPRAY A STINKY LIQUID FROM ITS TAIL WHEN IT FEELS SCARED OR ANGRY? PEW!

BUT A KIT CAN'T AIM WITH ITS STINKY LIQUID VERY WELL YET.
TIME FOR PRACTICE!

WHAT DO YOU CALL A BABY DUCK?
A DUCKLING!

A DUCKLING IS BORN WITH A SOFT LAYER OF FEATHERS.
IT CAN SEE AND HEAR VERY WELL, BUT IT CAN'T FLY YET.
IT NEEDS TO PRACTICE FLAPPING ITS WINGS TO GROW STRONGER.

DID YOU KNOW THAT A DUCKLING HAS FEATHERS THAT DON'T LET IT GET WET?
IT HAS A SPECIAL OIL ON ITS FEATHERS THAT MAKES THE WATER ROLL OFF.
QUACK!

A DUCKLING ALSO HAS A VERY CUTE VOICE.
IT CAN MAKE QUACKING SOUNDS TO TALK TO ITS FAMILY OR FRIENDS.
CAN YOU QUACK LIKE A BABY DUCK?

WHAT DO YOU CALL A BABY OWL?

AN OWLET!

AN OWLET IS BORN WITH A FLUFFY COAT OF WHITE OR GRAY FEATHERS.

DID YOU KNOW THAT
AN OWLET CAN TURN ITS HEAD ALMOST ALL THE WAY AROUND?
IT DOES THIS TO LOOK FOR DANGER OR FOOD.
HOOT!

AN OWLET ALSO HAS A VERY EXPRESSIVE FACE.
IT CAN MAKE DIFFERENT EXPRESSIONS WITH ITS EYES AND BEAK.
SOMETIMES IT LOOKS SURPRISED, ANGRY, OR HAPPY.
CAN YOU MAKE A FACE LIKE A BABY OWL?

WHAT IS A BABY DOLPHIN?
A DOLPHIN CALF!

A DOLPHIN CALF HAS A LITTLE HAIR ON ITS NOSE.
IT CAN SEE AND HEAR WELL, BUT IT CAN'T STAY UNDER WATER.
IT NEEDS TO COME UP FOR AIR.

DID YOU KNOW THAT A DOLPHIN CALF CAN MAKE NOISES AND FIND THINGS?
IT CAN GO CLICK-CLICK-CLICK AND HEAR THE ECHOES.
IT CAN USE THIS TO KNOW WHERE IT IS AND WHERE THE FISH ARE. CLICK!

A DOLPHIN CALF IS ALSO VERY SMART. IT CAN SWIM BEFORE IT IS BORN.
IT CAN ALSO COPY WHAT ITS MOMMY OR TRAINER DOES. WOW!

WHAT DO YOU CALL A BABY OTTER?
AN OTTER PUP OR KITTEN!

An otter pup is born with fur and whiskers,
but it can't swim or see anything just yet.
It needs its mommy and daddy to take care of it.

Did you know that an otter pup has a special pocket under its arm?
It can store its favorite rock or shell there.
It can use its rock or shell to crack open clams and mussels. Crack!

An otter pup also has a very playful personality.
It likes to slide on the mud, snow, or ice.

Can you slide like a baby otter?

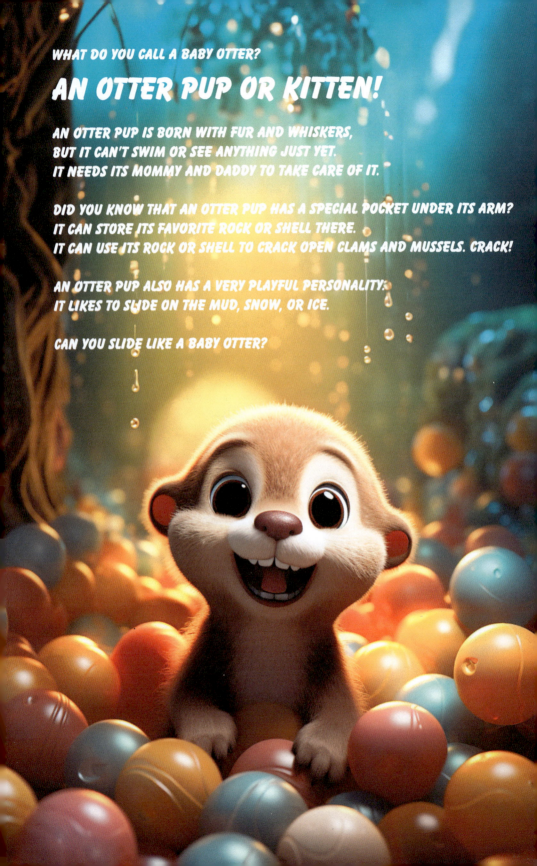

WHAT DO YOU CALL A BABY BAT?
A BAT PUP!

DID YOU KNOW THAT A BAT PUP CAN MAKE NOISES TO FIND THINGS?
IT CAN GO SQUEAK-SQUEAK-SQUEAK AND HEAR THE ECHOES.
IT CAN USE THIS TO KNOW WHERE IT IS AND WHERE TO FIND THINGS.
SQUEAK!

A BAT PUP ALSO HAS VERY LONG FINGERS AND A THIN SKIN.
IT CAN STRETCH ITS SKIN BETWEEN ITS FINGERS AND MAKE A WING.
IT CAN FLAP ITS WING AND FLY IN THE DARK. FLAP!

WHAT IS A BABY POLAR BEAR?
A POLAR BEAR CUB!

A POLAR BEAR CUB CAN'T SEE WHEN IT IS BORN.
IT CAN'T DO ANYTHING BY ITSELF. IT NEEDS ITS MOMMY.

DID YOU KNOW THAT A POLAR BEAR CUB IS VERY HUNGRY?
IT CAN DRINK A LOT OF MILK EVERY DAY.

A POLAR BEAR CUB ALSO HAS A LOT OF FUR.
IT CAN STAY WARM EVEN WHEN IT IS VERY COLD.
BUT SOMETIMES IT GETS TOO HOT AND NEEDS TO GET WET. SPLASH!

WHAT DO YOU CALL A BABY FLAMINGO?
A FLAMINGLET!

A FLAMINGLET IS BORN WITH WHITE OR GRAY FEATHERS.
IT CAN'T FLY YET, BUT IT CAN WALK AND RUN.

DID YOU KNOW THAT A FLAMINGLET HAS A SPECIAL MUSTACHE ON ITS NOSE?
IT HAS TINY HAIRS THAT HELP IT FEEL THINGS.
IT CAN USE ITS MUSTACHE TO FIND FOOD IN THE MUD OR WATER. SQUISH!

THE FLAMINGLET WILL TURN PINK WHEN ITS GROWS UP
BECAUSE IT EATS SO MUCH ALGAE AND SHRIMP! WHAT COLOUR WILL YOU BE?

WHAT DO YOU CALL A BABY PENGUIN?

A PENGUIN CHICK!

DID YOU KNOW THAT A CHICK CAN RECOGNIZE ITS PARENTS' VOICES AMONG THOUSANDS OF OTHER PENGUINS?
IT LISTENS FOR THEIR CALLS AND RESPONDS WITH ITS OWN.
SQUAWK!

A CHICK ALSO HAS A VERY CUTE WALK.
IT WADDLES ON ITS FEET AND SOMETIMES SLIDES ON ITS BELLY.
CAN YOU WADDLE LIKE A BABY PENGUIN?

WHAT DO YOU CALL A BABY BEE?
A BEE LARVA!

A BEE LARVA IS BORN FROM AN EGG LAID BY THE QUEEN BEE.
IT LOOKS LIKE A TINY WHITE WORM BEFORE IT TURNS INTO A BEE!
IT CAN'T SEE OR HEAR ANYTHING, BUT IT CAN SMELL VERY WELL.

CAN YOU SPOT A BEE LARVA
IN THE HIVE?
A BEE LARVA LIKES TO EAT
HONEY, POLLEN,
AND ROYAL JELLY.
YUMMY!

WHAT DO YOU CALL A BABY SLOTH?

A SLOTH CUB!

A CUB IS BORN WITH FUR AND CLAWS, BUT IT CAN'T WALK YET.
IT HANGS ON TO ITS MOTHER'S BELLY OR BACK
AND TRAVELS WITH HER IN THE TREES.

DID YOU KNOW THAT A CUB SLEEPS ALMOST ALL DAY?
IT DOES THIS TO SAVE ENERGY AND STAY WARM. ZZZZZ!

A CUB ALSO HAS A VERY ADORABLE SMILE.
IT ALWAYS LOOKS HAPPY AND RELAXED.
SOMETIMES IT EVEN GIGGLES WHEN TICKLED.
CAN YOU SMILE LIKE A BABY SLOTH?

WHAT DO YOU CALL A BABY BUTTERFLY?
A CATERPILLAR!

A CATERPILLAR IS A TINY CREATURE
THAT HATCHES FROM AN EGG.
IT HAS A LONG BODY WITH MANY LEGS
AND A PAIR OF ANTENNAE.

DID YOU KNOW THAT A CATERPILLAR
CAN TASTE WITH ITS FEET? STINK!
IT USES ITS FEET TO FIND THE RIGHT PLANTS TO EAT.
A CATERPILLAR ALSO HAS A BIG APPETITE.
IT EATS A LOT OF LEAVES ALL DAY
AND GROWS VERY FAST
BEFORE TURNING INTO A BUTTERFLY.
MUNCH!

DO YOU ALSO EAT LIKE A CATERPILLAR?
NOM!

WHAT DO YOU CALL A BABY OSTRICH?

AN OSTRICH CHICK!

A CHICK IS BORN FROM A VERY BIG EGG.
IT IS THE BIGGEST EGG IN THE WORLD!
IT HAS SOFT FEATHERS AND LONG LEGS, BUT IT CAN'T FLY AT ALL.

DID YOU KNOW THAT A CHICK CAN RUN VERY FAST?
IT DOES THIS BY EATING YUMMY THINGS LIKE PLANTS, SEEDS AND BUGS.
IT CAN GROW UP TO BE THE BIGGEST BIRD IN THE WORLD!
WOW!

A CHICK ALSO HAS A VERY FUNNY HABIT.
SOMETIMES IT PUTS ITS HEAD IN THE SAND
TO HIDE FROM DANGER OR TO LOOK FOR FOOD.!
DO YOU KNOW HOW TO PLAY HIDE AND SEEK?

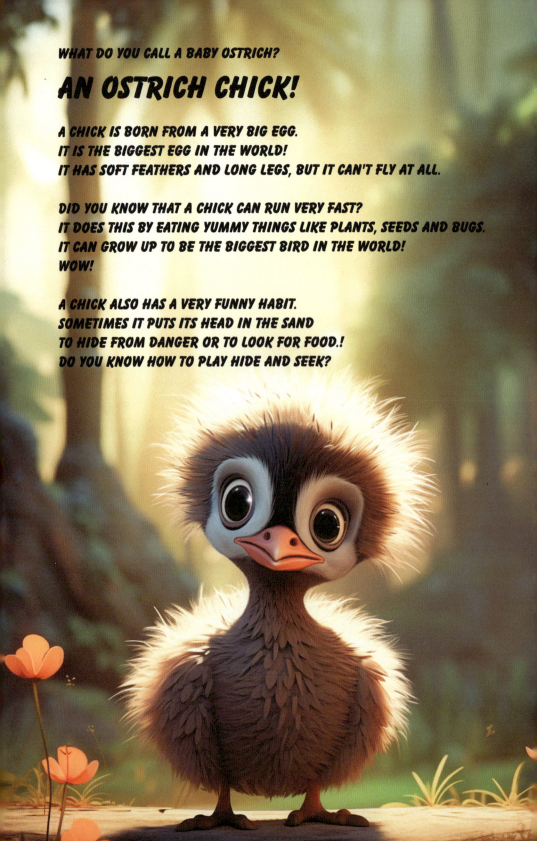

WHAT DO YOU CALL A BABY IGUANA?
AN IGUANA HATCHLING!

AN IGUANA HATCHLING IS TINY AND GREEN, BUT WATCH OUT!
IT WILL GROW UP TO BE BIG AND MEAN.
JUST KIDDING! IT'S NOT MEAN, IT'S NICE!

DID YOU KNOW THAT AN IGUANA HATCHLING
CAN CHANGE ITS COLOR LIKE A CHAMELEON?
THAT'S A COOL TRICK!

AN IGUANA HATCHLING ALSO HAS A LONG TAIL
THAT CAN SNAP OFF IF IT'S IN TROUBLE.
BUT DON'T FRET, IT CAN GROW BACK. THAT'S A HANDY SKILL!

WHAT DO YOU CALL A BABY CAT?

A KITTEN!

A KITTEN IS BORN WITH FUR AND WHISKERS,
BUT IT CAN'T SEE OR HEAR ANYTHING IN THE FIRST WEEKS.
IT NEEDS ITS MOMMY TO TAKE CARE OF IT.

DO YOU LIKE TO PLAY WITH TOYS?
SO DOES A KITTEN!
IT CAN USE ITS CLAWS TO SCRATCH THINGS
AND ITS TEETH TO BITE THINGS.

IT CAN ALSO USE ITS TONGUE TO GROOM ITSELF.
LICK! DO YOU BRUSH YOUR HAIR EVERY DAY?
A KITTEN LIKES TO EAT MEAT,
AND FISH BUT DOESN'T LIKE CHOCOLATE OR ONIONS. MEOW!
WHAT DO YOU LIKE TO EAT?

THIS IS THE END OF OUR BOOK OF BABY ANIMALS.
WE HOPE YOU HAD FUN AND LEARNED SOMETHING NEW.
THANK YOU FOR READING AND PLAYING WITH US.

IF YOU LIKED THIS BOOK,
PLEASE LEAVE A REVIEW AND TELL YOUR FRIENDS ABOUT IT.
YOUR FEEDBACK IS VERY IMPORTANT TO US
AND HELPS US CREATE MORE BOOKS FOR YOU.

THIS BOOK IS PART OF A SERIES CALLED ANIMAL WONDERS
A SERIES OF BOOKS ABOUT AMAZING AND ADORABLE ANIMALS.
HERE ARE THE OTHER BOOKS:

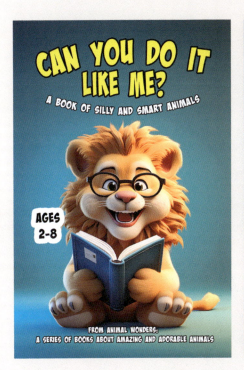
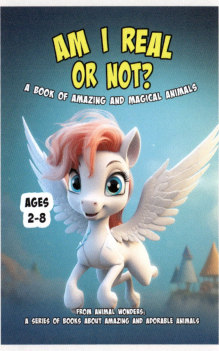

WE HOPE YOU WILL JOIN US AGAIN FOR MORE ANIMAL WONDERS!

HAPPY READING!

Printed in Great Britain
by Amazon